TERROR IN THE HEARTLAND: THE OKLAHOMA CITY BOMBING

John Hamilton

Published by Abdo & Daughters, 4940 Viking Dr., Suite 622, Edina, MN 55435.

Copyright ©1996 by Abdo Consulting Group, Inc., Pentagon Tower, P.O. Box 36036, Minneapolis, Minnesota 55435. International copyrights reserved in all countries. No part of this book may be reproduced in any form without written permission from the publisher. Printed in the United States.

Cover Photo by: Bettmann Archive.
Inside Photos by: Bettmann Archive: pp. 5, 20, 24.
Wide World Photo: pp. 7, 9, 11, 13, 15, 17, 19, 23, 27, 28.
Archive Photos: p. 10.

Edited by Bob Italia

Library of Congress Cataloging–in–Publication Data

Hamilton, John, 1959-
    Terror in the heartland: the Oklahoma City bombing / John Hamilton
        p.   cm — (Day of the disaster)
    Includes index.
    Summary: Surveys events surrounding the bombing of the Oklahoma City Federal Building including the rescue effort and the investigation by federal authorities.
    ISBN 1-56239-524-6
    1. Oklahoma City Federal Building Bombing, Oklahoma City. Oklahoma, 1995—
Juvenile literature. 2. Terrorism—Oklahoma—Oklahoma City—Juvenile literature.
3. Bombing investigation—Oklahoma—Oklahoma City—Juvenile literature.
[1. Oklahoma City Federal Building Bombing, Oklahoma City, Oklahoma, 1995.
2. Terrorism. 3. Bombing investigation.] I. Title. II. Series.
HV6432.H36 1995
364.1'64—dc20   95-23252
                                        CIP
                                        AC

CONTENTS

OKLAHOMA CITY: 1995

Target America

O n April 19, 1995, in Oklahoma City, Oklahoma, an explosion tore at the very heart of America.

It was the worst-ever terrorist attack on United States soil. At 9:02 a.m., a truck filled with nearly 5,000 pounds of explosives blew up in front of the Alfred P. Murrah Federal Building in downtown Oklahoma City. It turned the structure into a horrifying collection of rubble and twisted metal. One hundred sixty-eight innocent people died. Many of them were children.

The finger-pointing started almost immediately. The bombing had to be the work of Middle East terrorists. Or maybe it was drug bosses looking for revenge against the United States government. But two days after the explosion, the F.B.I. had a suspect. He was an American.

People across the nation were stunned. Many questions were raised. How could someone do this to his own people? How could someone hate our government so much that they would kill innocent people for revenge? How will the people of Oklahoma City deal with this terrible disaster? If this kind of thing can happen in America's heartland, is any place safe? How do we protect ourselves? And how can we keep our children sheltered in a world filled with hate?

Right: Rescue workers in a crane-supported basket survey the damage to the Alfred P. Murrah Federal Building in Oklahoma City, Oklahoma.

The Quiet Before The Storm

Here's the story of the terrible day of the Oklahoma City bombing—as told by a fictional paramedic on the scene.

"Bye Mom! Love you!"

I'll never forget those words. They were the last I heard my three-year-old son Josh say after dropping him off at America's Kids day care center in the Alfred P. Murrah Federal Building downtown. It was April 19, nearly 9:00 a.m. on a sunny spring morning. I was late for work. But I wasn't too late to give my kid one last hug good-bye. He wrapped his little arms around my neck. Then he gave me a squeeze before running off to play. I smiled as I watched him go. Soon all the kids would be sitting down for breakfast. They would be eating cereal and toast and opening juice cartons with their tiny fingers.

I turned and left. I knew I had found a safe place for my child. Finding good day care is hard, especially when your family does not have much money. I felt lucky getting Josh into America's Kids. The federal government managed it well. It was brightly lit. And it had lots of windows looking out from the second floor.

I hurried out to the parking lot and hopped in my car. As I drove off, I glanced at my watch and winced. It was 9:00 a.m. I was late for work at the hospital.

I'm a paramedic at St. Anthony's Hospital in Oklahoma City. I ride in an ambulance. It's my job to get sick or injured people stable (like stopping bleeding) and get them safely to a hospital. It can be a hard job sometimes. But it makes me feel good knowing I'm helping people. And the people in Oklahoma City are great.

The Alfred P. Murrah Federal Building

Bureau of Alcohol, Tobacco, and Firearms (ATF)

Secret Service

Drug Enforcement Administration (DEA)

Dept. of Housing and Urban Development (HUD)

HUD

DEA

Small Business Administration

U.S. Marine Corps Recruiting

Dept. of Agriculture   HUD   U.S. Customs

Dept. of Labor

Veterans Admin.

U.S. Dept. of Transportation

Snack Bar

U.S. Air Force

U.S. Army Recruiting

Health and Human Services

Dept. of Defense

Credit Union

U.S. Army

General Accounting Office

Day Care Center

Social Security Administration

This photo shows the location of the various government agencies in the demolished Murrah Federal Building.

The force of the explosion was felt 30 miles away, and caused damage four blocks in every direction. When the truck bomb went off, support columns at the front of the building were destroyed, causing the entire north side to collapse.

7

Josh's father, my husband Rick, is a lawyer for the U.S. Department of Agriculture. He works in the Federal Building. He usually brings Josh with him. Today, Rick was home with the flu. So it was up to me to get Josh to day care. It made me late. But my boss would understand.

Everybody in Oklahoma City is so nice. We've lived here all our lives. We're happy to raise our family in America's heartland. We don't have to worry much about gangs and shootings and other crimes. We're content here. We feel safe.

Explosion!

I thought of these things as I sat at the red light on Robinson Avenue, a block away from the Federal Building. I looked at my watch again. It was 9:02 a.m. I was really going to be late now. When the light finally turned green, I started to go. Suddenly I saw a bright orange flash in the sky. Then the Earth shook. A huge explosion nearly broke my eardrums.

I slammed on the brakes, then looked behind me. Through the back window, I could see a huge plume of smoke and fire rising hundreds of feet into the air. It looked like an atomic blast. Then it started raining glass and concrete. The debris fell all around the car. I heard it plunking down on my roof like a hard rain. I looked to my left and saw the First Methodist Church. All its windows were blown out.

At first I was so confused, I just sat there. Then I figured a gas pipeline had exploded. But where? I looked back through the window again. A cloud of black smoke billowed from a building somewhere behind me. *Behind me!* A shiver ran up my spine. Josh!

An unidentified woman calls out to friends as she waits for medical treatment following the truck bomb blast.

I got out of the car and stared at the black plume with a sense of dread. I started walking toward it. A woman in the car behind mine got out too. Her head was bleeding from a glass cut. I asked her if she was all right. When she nodded, I continued walking toward the smoke. Then I ran.

When I reached Fifth Street and rounded the corner, my whole body shook. In front of me was the Federal Building—or, what was left of it. Just minutes ago it was a proud nine-story building. Now the entire north side was gone. It looked like it had been ripped away by some evil giant.

Above: The explosion turned the Murrah Building into a twisted pile of concrete and steel.

Right: Rescue crews work together as they climb over areas of debris.

Strands of metal cable and concrete hung from the shattered floors. A huge pile of rubble settled at the base of the building, near the street. The whole structure hissed and belched. Black smoke and dust billowed into the Oklahoma sky. On the street, cars were overturned and crushed. Many were on fire. Parking meters were twisted and ripped from the ground. Shards of glass and hunks of brick were everywhere.

No gas explosion could have caused so much damage. It must have been a bomb. My mind was filled with a sickening mixture of fear and hatred. What kind of monster would do something like this? And why in Oklahoma City? This just doesn't happen here.

Then I noticed the toys. Their bright colors stood out against the grey mass of rubble. They were strewn all over. I just stood there, blinking. My mind wanted to turn itself off. But finally my lips formed a word. It snapped me out of my shock.

"Josh," I said softly.

My son was in there somewhere. "Josh!" I screamed, running toward the building.

Helping the Victims

I bumped into a man. His clothes were in shreds. The side of his head was covered with blood. "Can you help me, please?" he said politely. Then I noticed one of his arms was missing. He was in such shock that he didn't seem to notice. I sat him down, took off my jacket, and wrapped it around the wound. In the distance, sirens shrieked.

I helped the man with one arm lay down and told him not to move. I stood up just as the first of many ambulances, police cars, and fire trucks arrived. I turned toward the building again. Out of the smoke and haze,

Firefighter Skip Fernandez of Miami, Florida, rests his head on his search dog, Aspen, after finishing his 12-hour shift looking for survivors.

people slowly made their way out of the wreckage. Their clothes were tattered and blood-soaked. In the rubble pile I could hear people calling out for help.

"Ma'am, are you alright?" someone said.

I turned and found a fire department paramedic standing next to me.

"My son's in there," I replied, turning to look at the smoldering rubble.

"You need to leave," he said. "It's too dangerous here." The man took me by the arm to lead me away.

"Wait," I said, "I'm a paramedic too. I can help." I showed him my hospital badge. The man paused. Then he handed me some supplies from his medical kit. I took them gratefully. Then I headed back into the destruction, helping anybody I could find.

The next few hours are a blur to me now. The mother inside me wanted to run into the rubble, clawing at it with my bare hands to find my son. But then I'd find another victim who needed my help. I did what I've been trained to do.

The injuries were horrible. People had deep cuts, broken bones, and burns. At one point, I teamed up with another rescue worker. He'd been a medic in the Vietnam War. He told me he'd never seen anything as bad as this. It's like taking an office and putting it in a blender.

Sometimes my efforts were no use. I found one woman half buried in the debris. I held her hand for a few moments, and then she died.

Firefighter D.E. Jones rests on a sidewalk near the Murrah Building after putting in a long shift.

The Littlest Victims

The saddest part was the children. There was a police officer who arrived just after the blast. He ran up to the rubble after he heard a small cry for help. He pulled a one-year-old baby from the rubble. Then he handed the little body to a firefighter. The firefighter cradled the child as he rushed to a waiting ambulance. But it was too late. She was already dead.

Somebody took a picture of the firefighter holding the baby. It was on newspapers all over the world the next day. The photograph said a lot about how we felt that day: sorrow and despair mixed with the need to help.

We did find some children alive. They were walking around dazed, looking for their parents. But mostly we found dead bodies. One rescue worker found a dead child next to an American flag. He was so mad he was shaking. "Who would blow up babies?" he shouted to no one in particular. Later I saw him talking to a police officer.

"Find out who did this," he demanded.

Everyone I talked to was sure the bombing was the work of Middle East terrorists. Hatred was running high. I wasn't so sure. We shouldn't rush to judgment before all the facts are in. Innocent people can get hurt.

Later, Oklahoma's Governor Frank Keating said, "These people will never walk the Earth again if I have anything to do with it." But I wasn't thinking about revenge yet. I only cared about one thing: Josh.

I pressed on, helping where I could. I was trying to find a sign—any sign—of Josh. After the first hour, my mind grew numb from the pain and destruction around me. More and more rescue crews arrived on the scene to help. They swarmed over the rubble, hoping to find more

Rescue and emergency workers search through the rubble of the bombed-out Murrah Building. Despite cold and rainy weather, rescue efforts continued in hopes of finding survivors.

survivors. Dozens and dozens of nurses showed up. I found out later there was a nursing convention in town. When they heard about the bombing, they rushed to the scene to assist.

It seemed like all ambulance, fire and police squads in town were there to help. Rescue teams in protective gear and white helmets dug deeper into the shattered building. And there were many body bags with dead victims.

There was great danger just being there. We had to watch out for fire and poisonous gas. And there was always the danger that the rest of the building could crash down on our heads. In fact, a chunk of concrete did fall on one rescue worker. She died a few days later.

Rescue

There were some happy moments. We found a woman trapped in a small space between two collapsed floors. She was bruised and had cuts, but seemed okay. We worked hard to get her out. I stayed and held her hand as other rescuers worked to lift the heavy debris.

Just when we were ready to lift the last big piece, we were told to leave. Someone said there was another bomb about to go off. It was hard to leave that poor woman there in the rubble. Later, after they discovered there was no other bomb, they freed the woman. It took four hours to dig her out.

Sometimes the rescues didn't go so well. We found another trapped woman. Her right leg was pinned under a huge chunk of concrete. They couldn't move the slab. So a doctor had to cut off her leg below the knee to free her. It was the only way to get her out alive.

After a few hours, I was exhausted. I moved to a place about a block away where they brought the injured. Medical teams gave first aid before sending people to the hospitals. I looked into the faces of the injured. Some sat there holding bloody bandages, staring blankly into space. Others were laid out on stretchers, unmoving. But there was no Josh.

Finally, I lost control. I sat down on the curb and started crying. It was just too much for me to take.

But then, after a minute, I heard a little voice. I looked up and saw a firefighter carrying a little boy in his arms. It was Josh!

F.B.I. and military personnel search fields for evidence near the Murrah Building.

I ran to him, sobbing with joy. The policeman told me he'd found my son in the building's basement with a small group of other children. Josh's face was cut by broken glass, and his arm was broken. But he was alive.

I'll never forget that morning in Oklahoma City. How could anyone forget? I was lucky that day. I got my Josh back. But many, many families got only bad news. I hope they find the monsters who did this. I hope they lock them away forever, with the pictures of all the victims lining their cell. That way, they'll be reminded every day of the pain and suffering they've caused.

A woman consoles her son as they listen to the sermon at a memorial service held for the victims of the Murrah Building bombing.

The Investigation

(The story is picked up here by an F.B.I. special agent, writing a field report one month after the tragedy.)

It's May now, just over a month from the day the Federal Building was bombed. I'm returning to F.B.I. headquarters in Washington, D.C., tomorrow. I've taken field notes to help me piece together a final report. Here's what we know so far about this horrible disaster.

On April 19, 1995, at exactly 9:02 a.m., a truck bomb loaded with approximately 5,000 pounds of explosives ignited outside the Alfred P. Murrah Federal Building in downtown Oklahoma City, Oklahoma. The bomb was made from fertilizer and fuel oil. The truck was parked on the north side, within 15 feet (4.5 m) of the front of the building. The Murrah Building was built over 20 years ago. It was not made to withstand the force from such a blast. When the bomb exploded, support columns over the two-story entrance foyer collapsed. This caused the front of the building to cave in. Within a few seconds, floor slabs fell one on top of another. The bomb left a crater eight feet (2.5 m) deep and 30 feet (9 m) wide.

One hundred sixty-eight people died, including 19 children.

The explosion was so great that other buildings four blocks away were damaged. One of the most heavily damaged was the Y.M.C.A. and Day Care Center building across the street. Flying glass seriously injured many children.

The Murrah Building held several U.S. Government agencies. They included offices of the Bureau of Alcohol, Tobacco and Firearms (A.T.F.), the Secret Service, Drug Enforcement Administration (D.E.A.), and Social Security Administration. A day care center occupied the entire 2nd floor of the building.

Emergency response was fast and effective. Emergency workers were highly skilled. Shortly after the blast, many medical teams and emergency workers gathered at the scene. More than 600 firefighters searched through the rubble, looking for survivors and recovering the dead. Over 300 members of the Federal Emergency Management Agency searched crawl spaces and helped treat victims. Countless medical personnel and local police also helped.

The Oklahoma National Guard provided crowd control and assisted rescue workers. More than 1,400 Red Cross volunteers aided victims' families and helped feed rescue workers. Even the people of Oklahoma City helped. They held blood drives and gave food and supplies to victims and their families.

The F.B.I. Arrives

The F.B.I. arrived quickly on the scene. President Clinton called the terrorists "evil cowards." He authorized a full-scale investigation. Half of the F.B.I.'s 10,000 special agents went to work on the case. The A.T.F., state and local police assisted them. The investigation was larger than the one conducted when President John F. Kennedy was assassinated in 1963.

The F.B.I. calls these kinds of cases "major specials." They include such crimes as bombings, airline hijackings, and prison riots. We practice often to deal with these crimes. When word came of the Oklahoma City bombing, we knew exactly what to do. Within hours we were in the city. We set up a command post and began the investigation. Criminals almost always leave a trail behind them. We were ready to collect evidence.

Timothy McVeigh, prime suspect in the Oklahoma City bombing.

Clues

Our first break came almost right away. One of our agents found a twisted piece of metal two blocks from the blast sight. He recognized it as a truck axle. It still had the VIN (vehicle-identification number) stamped on it. Our computers traced the number to a Ryder rental truck from a shop in Junction City, Kansas, 270 miles from Oklahoma City.

We knew a Ryder truck was used to blow up the Murrah building. An automated teller camera at a bank across the street photographed a Ryder truck pulling up to the federal building minutes before the explosion. We immediately sent agents to Junction City to talk to the rental shop

Timothy McVeigh is led from the courthouse in Perry, Oklahoma, by F.B.I. agents and other law enforcement officers after being charged with involvement in the Murrah Building bombing.

employees. From their description, we made two drawings of our suspects. We called them John Doe No. 1 and John Doe No. 2. A $2 million reward for information was issued. Leads poured in. The F.B.I. hotline received 2,000 calls. Dozens of agents fanned out. They showed people drawings of the suspects.

Suspect Arrested

At the Dreamland Motel just outside of town, the owner recognized John Doe No. 1. The suspect had stayed at the motel a few days before the bombing. His name was Timothy McVeigh. At that time we didn't know that McVeigh was already in custody in an Oklahoma jail.

Just 90 minutes after the bombing, police in Perry, Oklahoma, stopped McVeigh for driving without a license plate. He was arrested after the police discovered he had a five-inch knife and pistol loaded with "cop killer" bullets. He was sent to the Perry jail.

Meanwhile, our computer checked on McVeigh. The F.B.I. has a huge computer network that lets us track suspects. Using this system, we discovered that McVeigh was in Perry. Authorities were called just 30 minutes before he was to be set free.

Guards escorted McVeigh from the Perry jail. Onlookers shouted "baby killer." A helicopter took him to Tinker Air Force Base. From there, he went to federal prison, where he awaits trial. If convicted, the government will seek the death penalty.

That same day, two friends of McVeigh, brothers James and Terry Nichols, were also arrested. McVeigh and the Nichols are connected to a right-wing paramilitary group called the Michigan Militia. Leaders of the Michigan Militia deny the suspects are members. But they have attended several meetings.

The motive for the bombing is still unknown. McVeigh, a former Gulf War veteran, remains silent. He considers himself a prisoner of war. We do know that he and the Nichols were secretive and obsessed with guns, and the tragedy in Waco, Texas. (Exactly two years to the day before the Oklahoma City bombing, four A.T.F. agents and more than 70 members of the Branch Davidian Cult were killed during a raid on their headquarters.) The exact connection between the suspects and the militia groups is not known at this time. So far, only McVeigh and Terry Nichols has been charged with the bombing.

Murrah Building Demolished

On May 23, 150 pounds of dynamite were used to bring down what was left of the Murrah Building. Earlier there had been talk of letting the building stand as a memorial to the dead. But the shell of the bombed-out building was too unstable and dangerous. Dynamite was placed in such a way that the center collapsed first, then the two sides. It took just seven seconds for the building to come down.

As of this writing, John Doe No. 2 is no longer a suspect. He was identified as an innocent bystander at the Ryder Truck dealer. But leads are still coming in of possible co-conspirators. The manhunt continues.

Helping Kids Cope

How do children react in the face of such terrible news like the bombing in Oklahoma City? Most likely you are angry, confused, and a little bit afraid. You might be thinking about the bombing without talking about it. But you should talk about it, especially with your parents. Tell them how you feel, ask questions. Your parents will take your fears seriously. They want to help you, reassure you.

And remember, it's okay to be angry. It's a normal feeling. But don't let your anger get so hot that you thirst for revenge and hurt somebody, even if you think you're right. Hurting other people never solves problems. It only leads to more pain.

After the bombing, President Clinton said, "My message to the children is that this was an evil thing, and the people who did it were terribly, horribly wrong. We will catch them, and we will punish them. But the children of America need to know that almost all the adults in this country are good people who love their children and love other children. And we're going to get through this."

Aren Almon of Oklahoma City clutches a teddy bear as she is greeted by President Clinton after a prayer service for the victims of the deadly truck bomb attack in downtown Oklahoma City. Almon's one-year-old daughter Baylee was killed in the attack.

Rescue workers stand together in front of the rubble of the Alfred P. Murrah Federal Building during a memorial service to remember those killed in the April 19, 1995, truck bombing attack.

REFERENCES

Alter, J. (1995, May 1). Jumping to conclusions. *Newsweek*, 55.

Associated Press (1995, May 11). Nichols charged in Oklahoma blast. *Minneapolis Star Tribune*, p. 2A.

Associated Press (1995, April 27). At school, kids talk, draw to ease fears. *Minneapolis Star Tribune*, p. 7A.

Barnes, E. (1995, May 22). Detours on the trail of the bombers. *Time*, 43.

Beck, M. (1995, May 1). 'Get me out of here!' *Newsweek*, 40.

Duffy, B. (1995, May 1). The end of innocence. *U.S. News & World Report*, 34.

Gibbs, N. (1995, May 1). The blood of innocents. *Time*, 57.

Gleick, E. (1995, May 8). "Something big is going to happen." *Time*, 50.

Gleick, E. (1995, May 1). Who are they? *Time*, 44.

LaCayo, R. (1995, May 8). A moment of silence. *Time*, 42.

Leland, J. (1995, May 8). 'I think about it all the time.' *Newsweek*, 35.

Leland, J. (1995, May 1). Why the children? *Newsweek*, 48.

Lemonick, M. (1995, May 1). How can young survivors cope? *Time*, 62.

Morganthau, T. (1995, May 1). The view from the far right. *Newsweek*, 36.

Morganthau, T. (1995, May 22). Scouring the west for the keys to the conspiracy. *Newsweek*, 26

New York Times (1995, May 4). Portrait is emerging of a silent and intense McVeigh. *Minneapolis Star Tribune*, p. 9A.

News Services (1995, April 28). An 'indelible trail of evidence' cited. *Minneapolis Star Tribune*, pp 1A, 9A.

News Services (1995, April 27). McVeigh told pal of 'something big.' *Minneapolis Star Tribune*, pp. 1A, 8A

Peter Jennings' Journal. (1995, May 5). Putting the past to rest in Oklahoma City. *America Online News*. [On-line]. Available: America Online: Author.

Reuters. (1995, May 4). OKBomb update. *America Online News*. [On-line]. Available: America Online: Author.

Reuters. (1995, April 26). Updates with possibility of 2nd suspect dead. *America Online News*. [On-line]. Available: America Online: Author.

Thomas, E. (1995, May 1). Cleverness—and luck. *Newsweek*, 30.

Thomas, E. (1995, May 15). Cracking down on hate. *Newsweek*, 20.

Thomas, E. (1995, May 8). The plot. *Newsweek*, 28.

Walsh, K. and McGraw, D. (1995, May 1). A strike at the very heart of America. *U.S. News & World Report*, 51.

Watson, R. (1995, May 1). It's a scary world. *Newsweek*, 53.

GLOSSARY

Alfred P. Murrah Federal Building

The Alfred P. Murrah Federal Building was constructed in Oklahoma City, OK, almost 20 years ago at a cost of more than $13 million. It housed 15 federal agencies, some defense-department offices, plus a day-care center. It was not designed to withstand the force of a bomb blast.

Fertilizer Bomb

A chemical called ammonium nitrate can be good or bad, depending on how it's used. When farmers spread the white crystalline compound on their fields, it works as a fertilizer that helps crops to grow. But ammonium nitrate also can be mixed with fuel oil to create powerful bombs, like the one used to blow up the Alfred P. Murrah Federal Building in Oklahoma City. It's difficult to get the right mixture needed for a bomb, but if a person has the experience and knowledge, it can be done.

First Aid

Emergency treatment given to sick or injured people before professional help from a doctor or paramedic is available. The first priorities include checking for breathing and heart beat, stopping severe bleeding, and treating for shock. Quick and proper first aid can mean the difference between life and death.

Militia

A military force made up of armed citizens, different from an organized regular army. Many militia members hold regular jobs, then train for combat in their spare time. Militias have their own goals. Many are opposed to the U.S. Government, especially the way the United States taxes its citizens, or the way in which federal land is managed.

Paramedics

Highly trained rescue workers who perform first aid on sick or injured people, then get them to a medical center as soon as possible, usually in an ambulance. Paramedics train for many weeks to handle all the different kinds of injuries they may encounter on the job.

Search Dogs

These dogs work with rescue teams to search for victims buried in the debris of collapsed buildings. They've been trained since they were puppies. When they sniff a human in the rubble, they scratch at the surface, alerting the rescue team that a survivor, or dead victim, has been found.

Shock

Shock resulting from an injury, sometimes called traumatic shock, is much different from electrical shock. In injury-related shock, body functions like blood pressure and breathing begin to fail and shut down in response to the injury. Shock can kill, and must be dealt with quickly. First aid for shock involves keeping the victim lying down, covering him enough to keep from losing body heat, and getting medical help as soon as possible.

Terrorists

Terrorists use violence, intimidation, and terror to achieve their goals, which are usually political. Since members of a terrorist group don't have enough members or weapons to win a war by themselves, they use terror on unarmed citizens, sometimes with the use of bombings or skyjackings. Their hope is that the citizens will become so afraid that they will demand their government give the terrorists what they want.

INDEX

BLUE'S FUNNY FRIEND GARDEN

You will need: grass seeds, dirt or potting soil, a paper cup, markers, water, and a sunny spot

1. Decorate the outside of your paper cup with a funny face.

2. Fill your paper cup with dirt or potting soil.

3. Push some holes into the dirt with your finger and drop a seed into each hole. Then cover the seeds back up with dirt.

4. Water your seeds when you plant them and then whenever the dirt is starting to get dry.

5. Watch the grass grow and grow! When the grass gets too long, you can tie it up with ribbon—or give your new friend a "haircut."

Thanks so much for your help today. As you can see, Blue's tomato soup is a big hit! And we even made a salad with the lettuce and the cucumbers that we picked. Bon appétit!